Mustang Horses

by Grace Hansen

Abdo HORSES Kids

Abdo Kids Jumbo is an Imprint of Abdo Kids
abdobooks.com

abdobooks.com

Published by Abdo Kids, a division of ABDO, P.O. Box 398166, Minneapolis, Minnesota 55439.

Abdo Kids Jumbo™ is a trademark and logo of Abdo Kids.

Printed in the United States of America, North Mankato, Minnesota.

052019

092019

THIS BOOK CONTAINS RECYCLED MATERIALS

Photo Credits: Alamy, iStock, North Wind Picture Archives, Shutterstock

Production Contributors: Teddy Borth, Jennie Forsberg, Grace Hansen
Design Contributors: Dorothy Toth, Pakou Moua

Library of Congress Control Number: 2018963351

Publisher's Cataloging-in-Publication Data

Names: Hansen, Grace, author.

Title: Mustang horses / by Grace Hansen.

Description: Minneapolis, Minnesota : Abdo Kids, 2020 | Series: Horses set 2 | Includes online resources and index.

Identifiers: ISBN 9781532185656 (lib. bdg.) | ISBN 9781532186639 (ebook) | ISBN 9781532187124 (Read-to-me ebook)

Subjects: LCSH: Mustang--Juvenile literature. | Wild horse--Juvenile literature. | Horses--Juvenile literature.

Classification: DDC 636.13--dc23

Table of Contents

Mustang Horses

Mustangs are horses that roam freely in the American west. The highest populations live in Nevada. But they are also in California, Oregon, Utah, Montana, and Wyoming.

Spaniards first brought horses to the **New World** in the 1500s. Many horses were left behind when the Spaniards were finished exploring.

Today, **descendants** of Spanish horses are known as mustangs. "Mustang" comes from the Spanish word *mestengo*. This word is used for wild or stray horses.

Mustangs have medium-sized bodies. They are often around 14.2 **hands** tall. They weigh between 600 and 800 pounds (272 and 363 kg).

2011

Mustangs have short backs.

Their tails sit low on their rounded **rumps**.

Their ears are short. Their narrow **muzzles** end in oval-shaped **nostrils**.

Mustangs come in many colors. But they are most often **sorrel** or **bay**. Their thick, wavy manes and tails tend to be black in color.

Personality

Training mustangs requires patience. Because they are **feral**, they tend to take some time to trust people.

Mustangs are smart and fearless. They are also very watchful. This is how they survived hundreds of years in the wild.

More Facts

- Mustangs travel long distances. Their hooves are harder and more durable than other horse breeds.
- Mustangs can survive on little food. They can even go many days without food or water if necessary.
- An elder mare is one of the leaders of the herd. She leads the pack away from any danger. She also brings the herd to water and food sources.

Glossary

bay – brown body color with black legs, mane, tail, and ears.

descendant – one who comes from ancestors.

feral – existing in a wild, natural state.

hand – a unit of measurement of a horse's height, equal to 4 inches (10.16 cm).

muzzle – the part of the head of some animals that contains the nose, jaws, and mouth.

New World – What North and South America were called by Europe after the early voyages of European explorers.

nostrils – two openings on the nose.

rump – the hind part of the body of a mammal.

sorrel – a light brown or reddish-brown color.

Spaniard – a native of Spain.

Index